Books in the Linkers series

Homes discovered through Art & Technology
Homes discovered through Geography
Homes discovered through History
Homes discovered through Science

Toys discovered through Art & Technology
Toys discovered through Geography
Toys discovered through History
Toys discovered through Science

Myself discovered through Art & Technology
Myself discovered through Geography
Myself discovered through History
Myself discovered through Science

Water discovered through Art & Technology
Water discovered through Geography
Water discovered through History
Water discovered through Science

First published 1996 A&C Black (Publishers) Limited
35 Bedford Row, London WC1R 4JH

ISBN 0-7136-4353 6
A CIP catalogue record for this book is available from the British Library.

Commissioned photographs by Zul Mukhida
Design by Jean Wheeler
Picture research by Liz Harman

Acknowledgements

Cephas; 7 (right), 9 (right), Chapel Studios; 12 (left), 20 (right), Eye Ubiquitous; 8, 10, 13, 18 (left),
22 (left), Positive Images; 2 (left), 9 (left), 11 (right), 14 (both), 15, 18 (right), 23, Tony Stone; Stephen
Johnson 5 (left), Michael Busselle 6, Gary Irving 7 (left), Paul Harris 11 (left), P H Cornut 17 (right),
Andrew Errington 20 (left), Robert Everts 21 and cover, James F Housel 22 (right), Wimpey Homes;
5 (right), Zefa; 2 (right), 4, 12 (right), 16, 17 (left), 19.

Printed and bound in Italy by L.E.G.O.

Homes

discovered through
Geography

Karen Bryant-Mole

Contents

A & C Black • London

Homes

Homes are places where people live.

People

Homes can be lived in by lots of people or just a few people. Some people, like this woman, live on their own.

Families

Many homes are homes for families. Some are homes for small families. Others, like the home in the picture above, are homes for large families.

Rooms

Homes are usually divided into rooms. There are often rooms for living in, cooking in, eating in, washing in and sleeping in.

How many people live in your home?
What sort of rooms does your home have?

In the town

Towns are places where lots of people live.
There are many different types of homes in towns.

Flats
Because so many people live in towns, lots of homes are needed.
More people can live in a particular space if homes are built on top of each other.

There are many homes in these blocks of flats.

Terraces

Some homes are built in rows, called terraces.

All the homes in a terrace are joined on to one another, so there is no wasted space between the houses.

Outskirts

There is usually more space on the edges, or outskirts, of towns. Houses are often larger, with bigger gardens.

Many are detached, which means they are not joined on to other houses.

Some are semi-detached, which means that one side of the house is joined on to another house.

In the countryside

Fewer people live in
the country than live in
a town.
Some people live in villages,
which are groups of homes.
Some people live in homes
that are far from any
other homes.

Cottages

Small homes in the country
are sometimes called
cottages.
There is plenty of space
in the country, so cottage
gardens are often large.

Farms

Most of the land in the country is used by farmers.

Their homes are called farmhouses.

Many farms, like the one below, have other buildings, such as barns and sheds.

Country houses

Very large homes are sometimes called country houses.

This house has been owned by the same family for many years. The man who owns it now was born here. So were his father and grandfather.

Conversions

Sometimes, homes are made from buildings that
were once used in other ways.
These homes are called conversions.

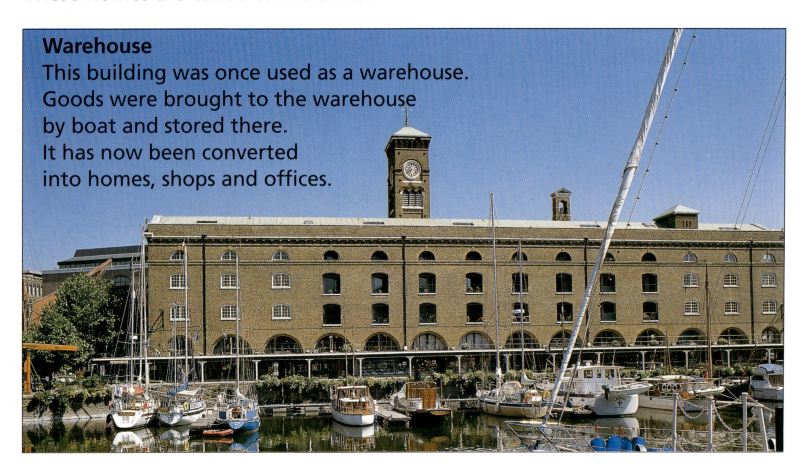

Warehouse
This building was once used as a warehouse.
Goods were brought to the warehouse
by boat and stored there.
It has now been converted
into homes, shops and offices.

Mill

The home on the right used to be a mill.
Mills used wind power or water power
to work machines.
Today, machines are powered by
electricity, so mills are no longer needed.

Barn

The home below is a barn conversion.
A few years ago, it would have had
cows trampling through it.

Why not find out whether any of
the buildings in your area have
been converted into homes?

Special homes

Some people live in
unusual homes.

Caravan
This home is called a caravan.

Some caravans can be moved from
one place to another but this sort of
caravan stays in one place.
The family who own it live in
their caravan all year round.

Canal boat
Some people live on boats.
The picture on the left shows
a canal boat.
The people who live on this boat have
a home that moves from place to place.

House boat
The picture below shows a house boat.
Unlike canal boats, house boats usually
stay in the same place all the time.

Moving home

People do not usually live in the same home all their life.

Reasons for moving

There are lots of reasons why people move home.

They may get a new job in a different town. Their home may be too big or too small.

Or, they may just feel like a change.

People often move into a new home after they get married.

Buying and renting

When people move home, there are lots of things to do.

People who own their home have to sell it and buy another.

People who rent their home have to find another home to rent.

Packing up

When everything is arranged, all the furniture and other belongings are packed up.

Then everything is put into a big removal lorry and taken to the new home.

Materials

The things that homes are made from are called materials.
A home is usually made from lots of different materials.

Plastic
The pipe below is made from plastic.
Plastic is waterproof and can be made into lots of different shapes.

Glass
Homes have glass in the windows and, sometimes, in the doors.
Glass is see-through.
It can keep out the wind and rain.

Bricks

Many homes have walls made from bricks. Most bricks are made from a special type of earth, called clay. Bricks are strong. Like glass, they keep out the wind and the rain.

Bricks, glass and plastic are all made by machines in factories.

Local materials

Around the world, lots of different types of homes are built. Many are made from materials that are found in the local area.

Mud and reeds
Homes made from mud and clay are found in many countries of the world. They often have a roof made from reeds or other plants. Homes like this are cheap to build.

Wood

The house below is built from wood.
Lots of trees grow in the surrounding area.
Wood is a useful building material.
It can be used for walls, roofs and floors.
It can be used to make furniture, too.

Ice

Homes can even be made of ice.
This sort of home is called
an igloo.
Nowadays, very few people
choose to live in an igloo.

17

Weather

The style of a house often depends on the local weather.

Rain
The home on the right is built in a country where it rains a lot.
It has a steeply-sloping roof, so that the rain can run off quickly and easily.

Cold
Homes in areas where it is cold and windy are often built with thick walls. This helps to keep the wind out and traps the warm air inside the house. They are often long and low, rather than tall and narrow.

Heat

In hot countries, many homes are built around a paved square, called a courtyard. The courtyard is usually nice and cool. There are always shady areas and there is plenty of fresh air.

Location

Where a home is, is called its location.
A home's location may affect the way it is built.

Earthquake
The homes on the right are built in a part of the
world where there are sometimes earthquakes.
New homes here are built in a special way, so
that they won't fall down if the ground shakes.

Water
Around the world, there are
many homes that are built
very near water or even
over water.
These homes are often built
on stilts.
Stilts help to protect the
homes from floods.

Mountains

Some areas of the world have lots of steep hills and mountains. Homes here have to be built into the sides of the mountains. They are often taller at the front than at the back!

Today's homes

Today, some homes are only found in one particular area.
But more and more homes are built in styles that are found all over the world.

Factories

Years ago, all the materials that were used to build houses had to be made by hand. Today, most building materials are made in factories, where machines make thousands of windows or bricks that are exactly the same size.

Transport

In the past, people had to make homes out of materials that were available nearby. Materials can now be transported all around the world by truck, boat and plane.

New homes

Here is a new home.
It is very difficult to guess in which part of the world it is being built.

Have a look at the homes near you.
Is there anything about them that makes them special to your area, or could they have been built anywhere in the world?

23

Glossary

converted changed from one thing into another
divided split up
local area the area close to where you live

rent pay someone money to live somewhere or use something
stilts tall poles
surrounding all around
transported carried

Index

How to use this book

Each book in this series takes a familiar topic or theme and focuses on one area of the curriculum: science, art and technology, geography or history. The books are intended as starting points, illustrating some of the many different angles from which a topic can be studied. They should act as springboards for further investigation, activity or information seeking.

The following list of books may prove useful.

Further books to read

Series	Title	Author	Publisher
Around the World	Houses Around the World	G. Hall	Wayland
Beans	all titles	various	A&C Black
Explainers	How Things Are Built	H. Edom	Usborne
Going Places	Where People Live	B. Taylor	A&C Black
My Book About	Houses and Homes	W. Jackman	Wayland
Our Country	all titles	various	Wayland
See for Yourself	Homes	Neil Morris	Wayland
Starting Geography	Houses and Homes	H. Barden	Wayland
Threads	Bricks	T. Cash	A&C Black
Topic Box	Houses and Homes	R. Nottridge	Wayland